One Christmas Day, Tim's presents were
a rocking horse,
an airplane,
a train,
and Rabbit.

Rabbit was his best present.
It had big, soft ears
and dark brown spots.

"Come on, Rabbit."

Off they went on the blue rocking horse.

"Faster, faster!" Tim laughed.

Up they flew in the yellow airplane.
Rabbit was the pilot.
"Let's go," Tim said.

Off they went on the red train.
"Rabbit, you're a real friend," Tim said.

One morning, Rabbit looked at Tim.
Mom looked at Tim.
"Oh, Tim! YOU have spots."

The doctor came.
"Tim, you are very sick. All your toys have to go!"

Mom put all Tim's toys in a sack.
She put the sack in the garden.

Rabbit was very cold and very sad.
But that night some real rabbits came.

Rabbit wanted to play with the rabbits.
"But I can't, I'm a toy," he said.

"You can!" a fairy said.
"You were real to Tim.
Now, you're a real rabbit!"

One day Tim said,
"Look, no more spots, Mom. Can I play in the garden?"

"Look Mom. That rabbit looks like my toy Rabbit. He has dark brown spots!"

Mom looked. "That's a real rabbit, Tim."
"My Rabbit was real to me," Tim said.

ACTIVITIES

BEFORE YOU READ

1. Look at the cover of the book. What can you see?
   (a) a gray rabbit with white spots.
   (b) a brown rabbit with dark brown spots.
   (c) a pink rabbit with white spots.

2. Look in the book. Can you find:
   a sack | a rocking horse | a fairy
   a real rabbit | a toy rabbit?

AFTER YOU READ

3. Look at the pictures of the toys in the story. Match the toy to the right color.

It's blue!
It's yellow!
It's red!

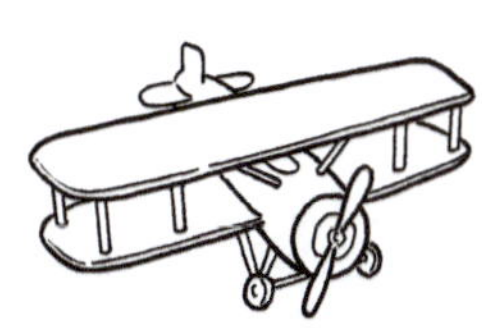

Pearson Education Limited
Pearson
KAO Two
KAO Park
Harlow
Essex
CM17 9NA

and Associated Companies throughout the world.

ISBN 9781292240039

This adaptation first published by
Penguin Books 2003
1 3 5 7 9 10 8 6 4 2

Adapted by Audrey McIlvain
Series Editor: Melanie Williams
Series created by Annie Hughes and Melanie Williams
Design by Shireen Nathoo Design

Printed in Brazil by Reproset RPPA 224575
SWTC/01

For a complete list of titles available in the Pearson Story Readers series please write to your local Pearson Education office or contact:
Pearson, KAO Two, KAO Park, Harlow, Essex, CM17 9NA

Answers for the Activities in this book are published in the free Pearson English Story Readers Factsheet on the website, www.pearsonenglishreaders.com